Red Clover & Meadow Vetchling

...nfrey   Red Campion
...se   Ox-Eye Daisy
...nesbill   Goat's Beard
...e   Nettle   Field Bindweed   Meadow Fescue

Freda Tuford

... Lea near Waltham Abbey in Essex during July & August

Here's Flowers for You

Here's Flowers for You

Freda Titford

ALLEN LANE · DAVID BATEMAN

DEDICATION

For Geoffrey & Richard

ACKNOWLEDGEMENTS

The flowers depicted in this book have either grown in my own or my friends' gardens, and without their generosity the work would never have been completed. My thanks are therefore due to the following people :- Janet Ambrose, Beatrice Butterswick, Rose Crispin, Olive Forde, Joan Harper, Olive Jones, Lorna Klagge, Edna Morris, Valerie Mottram, Anne O'Neill, Beatrice Pasmore, Meg Power, Eileen Taylor, Owen Thomas, Sis Ward and Hilda Wood.

Finally, for all the help and encouragement I received from them, I am especially indebted to Ron Treadgold, Michael White & Emma Wilson.

Allen Lane, Penguin Books Ltd.,
536, King's Road, LONDON, SW10 0UH
in association with
David Bateman Ltd.,
30-34, View Road, Auckland 10, NEW ZEALAND

First published 1982
Copyright © Freda Titford 1982
ISBN 0 7139 1490 4
Printed and bound by Dai Nippon Printing Co., HONG KONG

CONTENTS

Saxifrage umbrosa
LONDON
PRIDE

The William Morris Gallery
WALTHAMSTOW   LONDON

And there is pansies, that's for thoughts

HAMLET IV 5
WILLIAM SHAKESPEARE

INTRODUCTION

Wherever I have roamed in England, down a country lane, through towns and cities or the smallest of villages, there are reminders of former peoples; Anglo Saxon & Norman churches, palaces, manor houses, fortresses, windmills & a diversity of cottages to mention just some of our rich inheritance.

Quite often I have found alongside such legacies a wealth of flowers to enrich and soften man's work. Perhaps a large formal garden surrounding a manor house, a modest plot beside a cottage, a hanging basket outside a public house or maybe only a few wild flowers, but nevertheless they have added to my visual experience.

In this book I have tried to convey some of the enjoyment I felt when visiting such places in London, Essex, Kent & Sussex; by depicting the varieties of plants associated with each locality or building. It is a record of my personal journey through the parts of London & neighbouring countryside which I know and love.

It would have been over ambitious for the purposes of this my first book to have travelled to the remainder of the Home Counties, the East, West & North of England and even Scotland and Wales, for they too are all richly endowed with gems from our historic past and flowers of every kind. Perhaps in future publications I shall be able to include these equally beautiful and interesting parts of Britain.

Freda Titford   Autumn 1982 Chingford   London

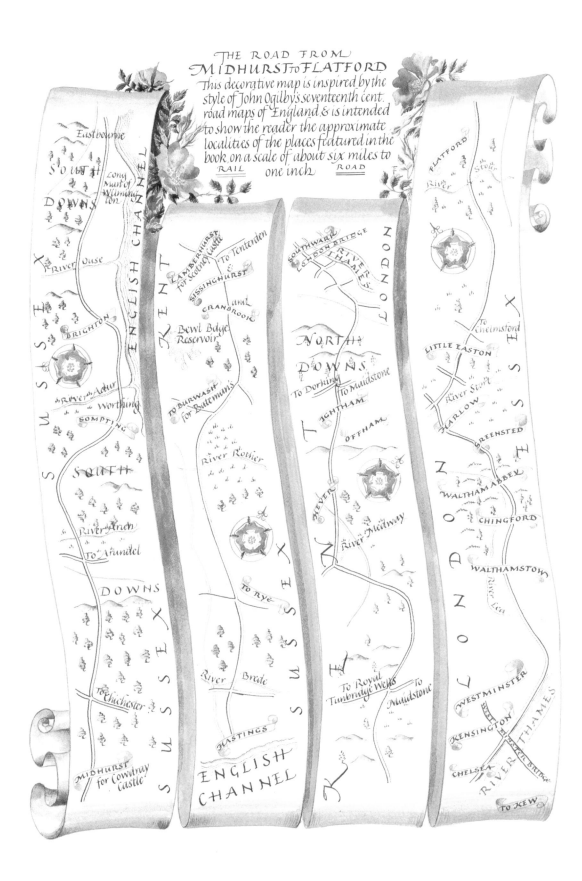

THE ROAD FROM
MIDHURST to FLATFORD
This decorative map is inspired by the
style of John Ogilby's seventeenth cent.
road maps of England, & is intended
to show the reader the approximate
localities of the places featured in the
book, on a scale of about six miles to
one inch

RAIL   ROAD

Eastbourne

SOUTH

DOWNS

Long Man of Wilmington

River Ouse

ENGLISH CHANNEL

SUSSEX

BRIGHTON

River Adur   Worthing

SOMPTING

SOUTH

River Arun

To Arundel

DOWNS

To Chichester

MIDHURST for Cowdray Castle

SUSSEX

KENT

LAMBERHURST for Scotney Castle   To Tenterden &

SISSINGHURST

and

CRANBROOK

Bewl Bridge Reservoir

To Burwash for Bateman's

River Rother

To Rye

River Brede

HASTINGS

ENGLISH CHANNEL

SUSSEX

SOUTHWARK

LONDON BRIDGE

RIVER THAMES

LONDON

NORTH

DOWNS

To Dorking   To Maidstone

IGHTHAM

OFFHAM

HEVER

River Medway

To Royal Tunbridge Wells   To Maidstone

KENT

Flatford

River Stour

To Chelmsford

LITTLE EASTON

River Stort

HARLOW

GREENSTED

WALTHAM ABBEY

CHINGFORD

WALTHAMSTOW

River Lea

WESTMINSTER

KENSINGTON

CHELSEA

RIVER THAMES

KEW BRIDGE

To KEW

ESSEX

LONDON

Here's flowers for you:

Hot lavender, mints, savory, marjoram;
The marigold, that goes to bed wi' the sun
And with him rises weeping... daffodils
That come before the swallow dares & take
The winds of March with beauty; violets dim,
But sweeter than the lids of Juno's eyes
Or Cytherea's breath; pale primroses
That die unmarried, ere they can behold
Bright Phoebus in his strength - a malady
Most incident to maids; bold oxlips and
The crown imperial; lilies of all kinds,
The flower-de-luce, being one!

'THE WINTER'S TALE'

WILLIAM SHAKESPEARE

9

Queen Elizabeth's Hunting Lodge
EPPING FOREST. CHINGFORD

10

The fine 15th century building known as Queen Elizabeth's Hunting
Lodge stands proudly on a hill overlooking Chingford Plain which
is part of Epping Forest. The lodge was one of Elizabeth the First's
favourite retreats, & in those days it was used more as a kind of grand-
stand from which the Sovereign could command the 'chase'.
Large bramble bushes abound on the Epping Forest plains and
their winter dress of red leaves & purple-red stems is most
attractive. Sometimes there is an added bonus.- a gorse bush
coming into bloom quite early in the year.

GORSE ulex europœus

BRAMBLE Rubus fruticosus

SWEET PEA
Lathyrus odoratus

FOXGLOVE
Digitalis purpurea

THE EAST END OF
WALTHAM ABBEY
FROM THE ABBEY GARDENS

Waltham Abbey in Essex is the oldest
Norman church in England, founded by
King Harold in 1060. Today only one
third of the building remains but the
majestic avenue of columns in the
nave give an impression of the great
Abbey as it was & also some inkling of the
mason's skill in the execution of their
decoration. Behind the east end of the
church where the monastic buildings
once stood there is now a rose garden,
arboretum, and a beautiful herbaceous
border

PURPLE LOOSESTRIFE Lythrum salicaria
MASTERWORT   Astrantia major

A walk along any of our inland
waterways will be most reward-
ing for the flower lover, & here
on the banks of the River Stort
there was plenty of one of my
favourite plants the Purple Loosestrife which like the Masterwort
thrives in moist conditions.
Between 1868 and 1911 this river
was owned by a private company
who worked the water mill. They
failed to keep the river navigable
and sold it to the Lee
Conservancy Board
for the sum of
five shillings!

HARLOW MILL
RIVER STORT, ESSEX

Cow Parsley   Coltsfoot   Dead Nettle

The immediate surroundings of Essex churches are often interesting both from the point of view of the wild flower enthusiast and the seeker of historical features. Here just outside Little Easton churchyard were the varieties of Spring wild flowers which one would expect to find growing in the stiff Essex clay and sharing pride of place with this 18th century stocks & whipping post. Until the middle of the last century the stocks were a feature of the English village scene. Miscreants were thus secured by their ankles whilst local residents meted out contempt and rotten eggs during the period of detention.

Wood Anemone

LITTLE EASTON, ESSEX — 18TH CENT. STOCKS

SWEET VIOLET , BRAMBLE
& LESSER CELANDINE

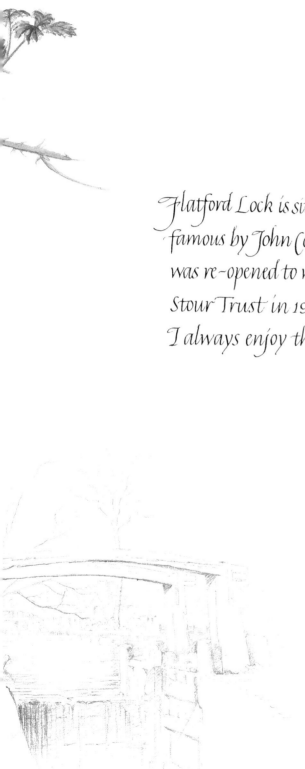

Flatford Lock is situated in Dedham Vale, made
famous by John Constable's paintings. The lock
was re-opened to waterborne traffic by the River
Stour Trust in 1975.

I always enjoy the sight of the yoke-like timber
lock lintels which were there
in Constable's time. They are
no longer required but have
been retained as a nostalgic
touch.

Another delight in Spring-
time is to find violets and
celandines growing either in
the shade of the brambles or
on the river bank.

FLATFORD LOCK

DEDHAM VALE ESSEX

GREENSTED CHURCH ESSEX

The churches of Saxon England were built
mostly of wood especially in Essex which
is virtually stoneless. The church of Saint
Andrew at Greensted-Juxta-Ongar is
well worth a visit; it is the only church in England which retains
its original nave of logs.
The lovingly tended church yard is planted with flowers & shrubs
and has a seat from which one can comfortably enjoy the peace &
Quiet.

CYDONIA JAPONICA & EVERLASTING PEA

HIMALAYAN BALSAM

Impatiens roylei

IGHTHAM MOTE

KENT

This small medieval manor house set in lovely meadowland is con-
sidered to be the most complete of its kind in the country. It is en-
circled by a moat & in the fine wooded grounds there is a tree-
fringed lake. With this plentiful supply of water it was not
surprising to find an abundance of the Himalayan Balsam,
or Policeman's Helmet attaining six feet or more.

20

JAPANESE AZALEA

SCOTNEY CASTLE
KENT

Scotney Castle was built in 1387. It has a spectacular round tower rising from a lake of lilies, and a moat reputed to be haunted by an 18th. cent. revenue man. The adjoining modern portion is a Gothic revival house of 1837. commanding a view of a wooded valley & extensive gardens filled with exotic trees and shrubs. The acid soil favours the growth of masses of beautiful rhododendrons and azaleas

Bramley Apple Blossom

Union Smock Mill, C R A N B R O O K . Kent

Few buildings add as much atmosphere to the English countryside as a windmill. This one is the noblest Smock mill in the country towering 75 feet above the town, it is one of our tallest mills. Built in 1814, it was in constant use until some thirty years ago and has been maintained in excellent repair by its mill owners.

SISSINGHURST CASTLE
KENT

In 1550 Sir John Baker built this castle
on the site of a fortified manor house For
some considerable time the house & park
were in ruins Fortunately in 1930 it was
rescued by Sir Harold Nicolson & his wife
Vita Sackville-West who created its world famous
gardens. The White Garden which contains grey and
white plants is divided by low neatly trimmed box
hedges & contrasts with the delightful Cottage Garden
where the colours are bright & warm and is planted with 'controlled
untidiness'. On the walls of the enclosed gardens which surround
the ruins of the old castle & its gatehouse buildings, roses and
clematis scramble with gay abandon.

ROSA
Mermaid'

CLEMATIS
Viticella

Mullioned window
Hever Castle

Syringa vulgaris
L I L A C

HEVER CASTLE
KENT

Although this is one of the smallest of our great houses it is one of the most romantically
beautiful. The ornamental gardens constitute a perfect setting for this fortified Tudor dwelling
house, once the home of the Boleyns. After Anne Boleyn was beheaded it was seized by Henry VIII.

Wallflower   Forgetmenot   Lily of the Valley

THE VILLAGE GREEN

OFFHAM KENT

The secluded Kentish village of Offham is set in a region of orchards and on the edge of the hop gardens. On the triangular village green is a unique feature, the only one in England, a Quintain. This medieval device afforded a sport in which the youth on horseback ran at it as fast as possible and attempted to hit the 'target' (the sixty-dot domino) with much force. Great swiftness & agility were then required in order to escape being struck on the back of the head by the bag of sand which instantly swung round from the other end. A gentler version of this old sport is revived each May Day using a bucket of water.

Golden
Yellow
Petals

Dark centre
Green + Brown

Dk Grn

Light Green

Cobalt Green

Yellow

Shirley
Poppy
Seed
Head
ab size

Sunflower
Side View

Sunflower 8'9 tall

⅓ actual size

7/2/9

30

SUNFLOWER
Helianthus Annus

COWDRAY CASTLE
Sussex

In 1793 a family curse was fulfilled when Cowdray Castle was consumed by fire This once majestic 16th century fortified manor house was for a time owned by Sir Anthony Browne a favourite of Henry VIII. Under the shadow of the castle ruins are the polo grounds where Prince Philip used to take part in polo matches.

The tall black net
shops are unique
in this country &
have been a feature
of Hastings since
the days of Elizabeth I.
They vary in height, the
tallest have three stories & are
about thirty feet high.
The remaining forty three
shops are still used for storing
nets and stand high
and dry on the beach
above sea level, where I was
thrilled to find the bright gold
Corn Marigold anchored in the sand.

CORN MARIGOLD   Chrysanthemum segetum

COMMON SORREL   Rumex acetosa

BATEMAN'S SUSSEX

Rudyard Kipling
lived in this three
hundred year old house, with its grey stone walls
for some thirty years. It is a notable example
of the country style of the Jacobean period.
Looking out from its windows one can
catch the glint of the stream flowing across the grounds,
the pear walk, & the tree-shadowed sunlit lawns.

MULLEIN Verbascum

TWO SUSSEX
COTTAGES & HYDRANGEA WITH HYPERICUM

ORIENTAL POPPY

YPRES TOWER at Rye in Sussex, built as a fort
in 1250. was burnt by the French in 1377. Later it
was sold to John de Ypres who gave it its name.

THE ROYAL BRIGHTON PAVILION . SUSSEX

The Royal Brighton Pavilion built for George IV about 1795 is one of the most remarkable buildings in England. Much of the interior is decorated & furnished in a realistically Chinese style & although the pavilion is mostly surrounded by a lawn and trees, I felt that if it had been planted with flowers, the gardener would surely have chosen the elegant Chinese Peony

CHINESE PEONY

JASMINE   Jasminum nudiflorum
PERIWINKLE   Vinca minor
SNOWDROP   Galanthus nivalis

The village of Sompting
with its church was one
of hundreds of settlements
founded by the Saxons.
As evidence of their
architectural skill the tower

of Sompting
Church with its
'German helm' pattern
roof has survived for
a thousand years.

FUCHS

MALL

London fortunately possesses a great many green spaces where people can walk or rest, away from the roar and smell of traffic. St. James's is one of the smaller of London's Royal Parks, but nevertheless, very popular with visitors. Some of the regulations of the Royal Parks make amusing reading. I quote, 'No stage coaches may be driven inside their limits, and while cycling is permitted on perimeter roads, it is only on condition that the rider is not cycling furiously. Horse-riding is allowed on specified paths, but no mules, asses or donkeys.'

St. James's Park
LONDON

lybrids
atera Loveliness'

43

THE ROYAL CHELSEA HOSPITAL

LONDON

The hospital was designed by
Sir Christopher Wren and
founded by Charles II in 1682
as a home for army pensioners.
They are easily recognised in their
scarlet summer coats, and three
cornered cocked hats worn only
on special occasions. Every May
the hospital grounds become a
mecca for flower lovers who flock
to the Chelsea Flower Show.

ROSA Peace'

DELPHINIUM Elatum

KEW

GARDENS

The Griffin of Edward III, one of the ten Queen's Beasts
which stand in front of the Palm House in Kew
Gardens. The beds of bearded Iris are stunningly
beautiful in May and June, and I was fortunate
to be given these two Kew Hybrids to paint by
one of the Gardens' botanical artists.

BEARDED IRIS

Ancient Egypt

46

'CHOKUSHI MON'

Standing on a small mound
in Kew Gardens there is this
replica of a famous Japanese gate called 'The Gateway
of the Imperial Messenger'.

BEARDED IRIS

Heather Hawk

47

SCABIOUS

'Clive Greaves'

CROWN IMPERIAL

Fritillaria imperialis

Daffodils 'Golden Harvest' & Crocus Tomasinianus

PELARGONIUM
ZONALE

Buckingham Palace is the
London home of the monarch.
Built originally in 1703 for the
Duke of Buckingham and
bought some sixty years later by George III, it has been crown property ever since. In 1913 this imposing
east front which faces the Mall was reconstructed to the design of Sir Aston Webb. This is the view of the
palace which the public see from Mall, and where they gather in their thousands to cheer the Royal
Family when they appear on the balcony for Royal Occasions During the celebrations for the wedding
of Prince Charles & Lady Diana Spencer it was gratifying to learn that not one flower in the Mall
was trampled on by the crowd of about half a million visitors.

Sir Christopher Wren designed
the summer house in Kensington Gardens in the early eighteenth
century for the personal use of Queen Anne, so that she might enjoy
the pleasures of the park. When George II opened Kensington Gardens
to the public he did so on condition that visitors wore "formal dress",
and later, William IV made matters more confusing by insisting on
respectable dress. Samuel Pepys records in his diary coming finely dressed to the park.

Magnolia Soulangeana   KENSINGTON GARDENS, LONDON

THE GEORGE INN, LONDON

The 'George', hidden away in a yard on
the southern side of London Bridge is
the only surviving medieval hostelry
in London which retains some of its
original features & is still used as an
inn. The double-tiered open wooden galleries lead to the
quaint old guest chambers and as one looks down into the yard below it
is easy to imagine the atmosphere in the days of the stagecoach with
travellers, coachmen, carriers, ostlers, horses and of course the 'boots'.

BEGONIA Tuberhybrida

Bellis perennis DAISY